THE CAMERA

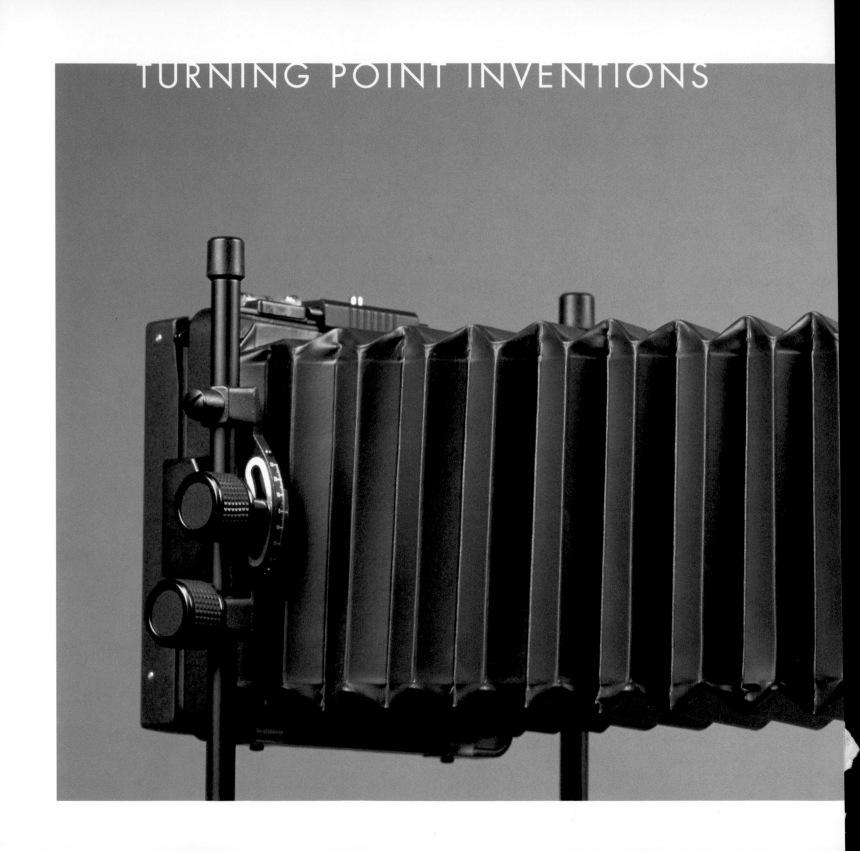

TURNING POINT INVENTIONS

THE CAMERA

JOSEPH WALLACE
Foldout illustration by Toby Welles

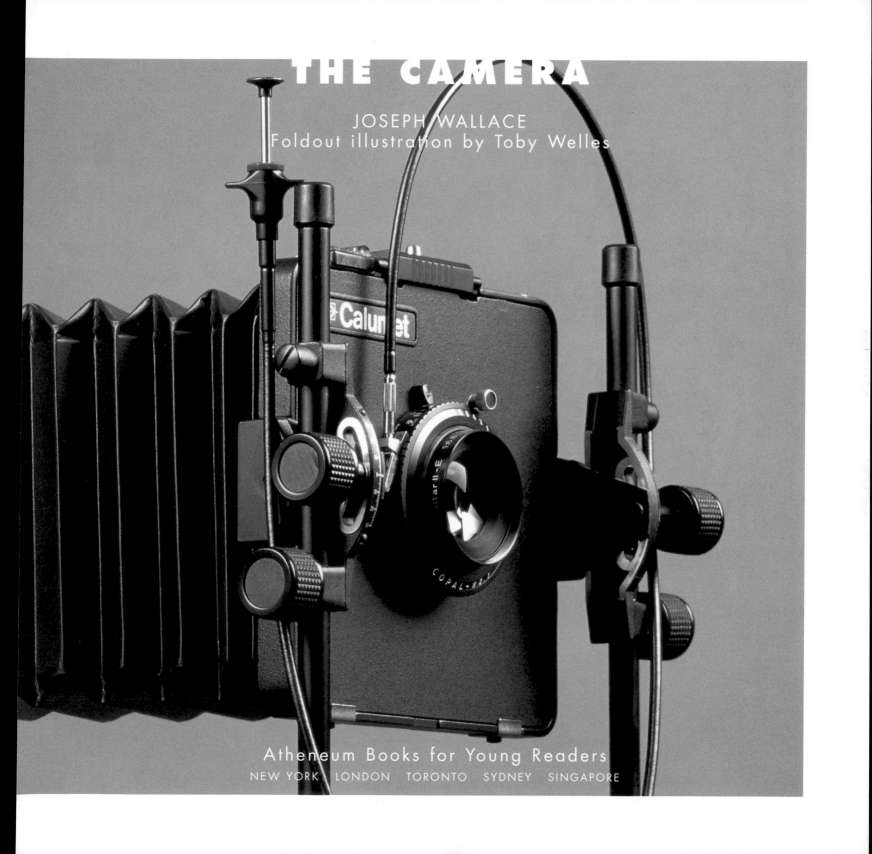

Atheneum Books for Young Readers
NEW YORK LONDON TORONTO SYDNEY SINGAPORE

Atheneum Books for Young Readers
An imprint of Simon & Schuster
Children's Publishing Division
1230 Avenue of the Americas
New York, New York 10020

FIRST EDITION

Produced by
CommonPlace Publishing
2 Morse Court
New Canaan, Connecticut 06840

Copyright © 2000
by CommonPlace Publishing LLC

Art Director: Samuel N. Antupit
Editor: Sharon AvRutick
Picture Research: Jean Martin
Production Design: Cheung/Crowell Design

Printed in Hong Kong through Global Interprint

10 9 8 7 6 5 4 3 2 1

ISBN 0-689-82813-6

Library of Congress
Card Catalog Number: 99-65243

Endpapers
Positive and negative images of "Kodak self-portrait with lillies" by Max Burgel, 1939.

Page 1
George Eastman popularized photography through his business acumen. His technical expertise made the camera simple enough for everyone to enjoy.

Pages 2–3
The Calumet professional studio camera, manufactured in the Netherlands in 1992, uses 4 by 5 inch sheet film.

Picture Credits

Archive Photos: pages 17, 22, 23(all), 41 (both), 47(left), 61(right);

Brompton Picture Library: pages 14, 25, 27, 34, 35, 36(right), 42, 43, 46(left), 58(left), 66(both), 67.

George Eastman House, Rochester, NY: pages 1, 10, 12, 28, 30, 31, 33, 36(left), 38, 47(right), 48, 55, 56, 58(right), 61(left), 62(right), 63(left).

Copyright © Harold and Esther Edgerton Foundation, 1999, courtesy of Palm Press, Inc.: page 70.

Bob Feather: pages 2–3.

Gernsheim Collection, Harry Ransom Humanities Research Center, The University of Texas at Austin: pages 6, 19, 20, 21, 32(both), 39, 44.

JVC Company of America: page 76.

Library of Congress: 40(right), 46(right).

Polaroid Corporate Archives: page 68(both).

Reuters/Masaharu Hatano/Archive Photos: page 75.

Private Collections: endpapers, pages 60, 62 (left), 63 (right), 64, 65, 74.

Superstock: pages 40(left), 69, 73(both), 77; Museo del Prado/Madrid: page 9; South Africa/Holton Collection: page 8.

Original art by Toby Welles and Anthony Bari: pages 49–54.

CONTENTS

1

BEFORE THE CAMERA

What did George Washington look like? The truth is, we don't really know. All the portraits we have of the "father of our country" are paintings that show Washington as a serious-looking man wearing a wig. At best, these images tell us how an artist saw Washington, not necessarily what you would actually have seen if you'd had the chance to meet the first president of the United States.

Another question: What did Abraham Lincoln look like?

This question we can answer, because we can trust what the portraits of the sixteenth president show us. That's because many of the surviving depictions of Lincoln are photographs, not paintings. By the time Lincoln took office in 1861, a group of brilliant inventors had created the first cameras, and, just as importantly, they'd also invented the first processes to capture images on photographic plates or paper.

Photographs — of our friends, family, sports heroes, favorite movie stars, and musicians — are all around us. Our books, our magazines, our lives are filled with their sharp, colorful images.

Yet less than 150 years ago, photography as we now know it didn't exist. The idea that someone could pick up a small box, aim it, push a button, and

Opposite
The first camera, the camera obscura, was nothing more than a dark room (in this case, a tent) within which images would be produced by light shining through a small opening. Artists could trace the images, producing more realistic scenes than were possible before.

capture the image of a face or a landscape forever would have seemed like a magic trick, not an art easily available to all.

Long before the invention of the camera, humans had a powerful desire to capture images of the world around them. As many as fifty thousand years ago, ancient people were already carving pictures onto animal bones. About fifteen thousand years ago, the human drive to reproduce the objects in our world led to a great flowering of paintings on the walls of some caves in Europe. Here, prehistoric artists created pictures of the animals they watched

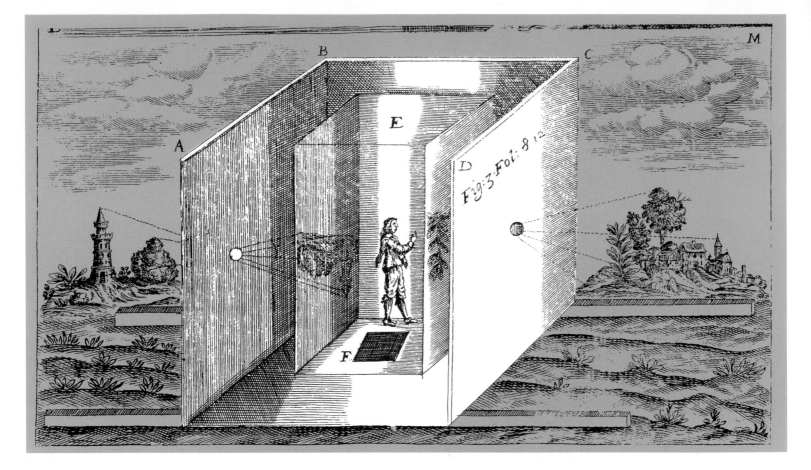

This camera obscura (shown here without its top or front) could be taken apart and moved from place to place. The artist would step inside the "darkened room" through a trapdoor and would then trace the images of the tower or village scene projected through the holes on either side.

and hunted: bison, horses, cattle, deer, and others. In many cases, these animals were so carefully and accurately painted that they are studied by today's scientists for clues as to how ancient animals looked and moved.

Why did these artists take the time and make what must have been a great effort to create such beautiful and detailed cave paintings? And why, in the thousands of years since those first primitive works of art, have humans in every culture on earth continued to depict the objects in their world?

According to photography historian Arthur Goldsmith, there are both complex and simple reasons for people to copy their surroundings. "Making pictures of the world of visible reality and of the dreams and visions in our heads is a way of relating ourselves to existence, to express our feelings about it, and to attempt to understand and control it," Goldsmith explains. But, he adds, "Even more fundamental, perhaps, it is an intrinsically satisfying act." In other words, we draw and paint because doing so makes us happy.

Still, as every amateur artist knows, drawing and painting can be a frustrating way of trying to reproduce the world with any accuracy. Throughout history, artists have had particular problems with capturing accurate perspective — reproducing the depth of a three-dimensional landscape's hills, trees, and distant horizons in the two dimensions of paper or canvas. Aristotle in ancient Greece and the Arabs around A.D. 1000 were familiar with the principle of what we now call the camera obscura (Latin for "darkened room"). It was probably an accidental discovery. A small opening in a darkened room projected an upside-down image of the outside world on an opposite wall. Sunlight filtering through leaves in a dark forest projected an image of foliage on the ground. Sometime during the sixteenth century these divergent bits of information were put together to make a small box which became the first camera obscura. The great Italian artist and inventor Leonardo da Vinci was so fascinated by the camera obscura that he described it twice in his notebooks. "When the images of illuminated objects pass through a small round hole into a very dark room," Leonardo wrote, "you will see on the paper [or on the opposite wall of the room] all those objects in their natural shapes and colors."

It was true. Light passing through a small enough hole (such as a pinhole) projects a detailed — though upside-down — image of an outside scene onto a wall, screen, or other surface in a dark room. A larger hole produces a larger but vaguer image. If the hole is too big, though, all that is projected is a patch of light in the shape of the hole itself. By late in the sixteenth century a basic type of camera obscura was being used by some painters to establish a realistic sensation of depth in their paintings.

A later refinement was made by placing a small lens in the hole to produce

a sharper image. Different designs evolved. In addition to what was considered the traditional box, a tent form was designed that allowed an artist to sit comfortably and sketch a large image.

By the eighteenth century, the camera obscura had shrunk enough that it hardly looked like a "darkened room" at all. Smaller versions fit inside wooden boxes that could be carried under an artist's arm. They contained a lens in the front that focused the image onto a screen made of ground glass (glass etched or scraped so that its surface becomes semitransparent, allowing it to display the image clearly) in the back of the box. Serious artists used completely clear glass and tracing paper. Ground or etched glass was frequently a later addition for demonstration purposes. Many models were completely portable.

In another important advance, a mirror was added behind the lens, which reflected the image onto a piece of paper or a ground-glass screen on the top of the box. This image was right-side up and on a horizontal surface, which made it far easier for an artist to trace it accurately. Later improvements included an adjustable lens (to allow focusing) and an iris diaphragm. This was made up of overlapping metal blades that would contract over the lens surface (much as the iris of the eye does) to regulate the amount of light allowed to hit the paper or screen, sharpening the image even further.

By the eighteenth century the camera obscura was, in fact, almost a camera. Its major drawback was that it lacked some automatic way of recording the images being let in through the hole — some way, in the words of a man named William Henry Fox Talbot, to use the sun's energy to preserve the camera obscura's "fairy pictures, creations of a moment, and destined as rapidly to fade away."

Early in the 1800s, Talbot and a few other brilliant inventors began to think that this seemingly magical possibility might be something they could actually achieve. They had the basics of a camera. Now it was time to invent photography.

Opposite
The camera obscura eventually began to resemble a camera in many ways. All that was needed was a way to preserve the images being projected inside the box.

2
THE PIONEERS

When a handful of inventors decided in the early 1800s that it might be possible to spread some chemicals on a piece of paper and in this way permanently capture an image projected by a camera obscura, their theories must have seemed ridiculous. But these inventors were completely serious. They were positive that the seemingly magical act of preserving an image on paper was possible.

In the 1720s, the German scientist Heinrich Schulze had shown that some naturally occurring chemicals (all of which were comprised in large part of powdered silver compounds) would darken when exposed to light. Before Schulze's studies, it had been believed that these changes were due to heat. Yet it wasn't until 1802 that a British man named Thomas Wedgwood thought to use this phenomenon to try to make pictures.

Wedgwood's father, Josiah, was a famous potter who used a camera obscura to help him create complicated designs on his pottery. Thomas felt that he could go one better, as a friend of his, the chemist and inventor Humphry Davy, wrote in an 1802 journal article. "White paper, or white leather, moistened with a solution of nitrate of silver, undergoes no change when kept in a dark place; but, on being exposed to the day light, it speedily changes color,"

Opposite
Few could believe what Louis Jacques Mandé Daguerre had done when he invented the kind of photograph called the daguerreotype, which some called "the mirror with memory." This daguerreotype is of Daguerre himself.

15

Davy explained. "Outlines and shades of paintings on glass may be copied, and profiles of figures procured, by the agency of light."

Specifically, when the coated paper or leather was placed behind a painting on glass and exposed to the sun, "the rays transmitted through the differently painted surfaces produce distinct tints of brown or black," Davy wrote. These tints differed in darkness depending on the colors of the picture itself. The coated paper stayed lightest where the dark tones of the picture prevented much light from coming through the glass and turned black where the sun struck it directly.

In other words, the coated paper produced a negative photographic image of the painting on the glass above. Unfortunately, the same technique did not work when the inventor tried to capture images from life, rather than from paintings. The image projected by the camera obscura was too faint to make any impression on the paper.

What's more, there was no way to prevent the image from darkening further on exposure to more light — Wedgwood could not "fix" it once it had reached the right levels of darkness and light. As Davy explained, "The copy of the painting, or the profile, immediately after being taken, must be kept in an obscure [dark] place. It may indeed be examined in the shade but, in this case, the exposure should just be for a few minutes." Even then, the image would gradually darken, until soon it looked like nothing more than a picture of a black night.

Thomas Wedgwood must have realized that some way would have to be found to make the images truly permanent, but he died in 1806, before he had the chance to search for a solution. Those efforts were left to a French inventor named Joseph Nicéphore Niepce, pronounced "Nee-eps." Working in a small house in Le Gras, France, Niepce too became interested in trying to use paper coated with silver compounds (called silver chloride or silver salts) to reproduce images from life. Unlike Wedgwood, though, Niepce strove to be able to produce paper sensitive enough to detect the faint images projected by the camera obscura. In 1816 he also built a camera that would make this more likely by casting a stronger image on the paper. In a letter to his brother Claude, he called his first try an "artificial eye, which is nothing but a small box six inches square; the box will be equipped with a tube that can be lengthened, and will carry a lenticular glass [lens]."

When this camera broke, Niepce wasn't discouraged. To replace it, he used a jewel case and the lens from a microscope to build the world's first miniature camera, just one and one-half inches square. He then placed this camera in his attic workroom, facing the window, so that it projected an image of a nearby birdhouse onto a piece of coated paper. "I saw on the white paper all that part of the bird house seen from the window," he wrote to Claude. "The background of the picture is black, and the objects white, that is, lighter than the background."

Niepce had produced the first photographic negative of the real world, a picture that was perfectly accurate, except that the dark tones of nature were represented as light on the paper, and the areas of greatest brightness appeared as dark patches. What's more, he was even able to partially fix the image — keep it from darkening — by washing it in nitric acid.

Even so, Niepce himself was skeptical of his achievement and unimpressed by the image. "The effect would be still more striking," he told his brother, "if the order of the shadows and the lights could be reversed." Unfortunately, though, Niepce never figured out how to produce a positive image from his negative one. Neither was he able to figure out how to make additional copies from his original.

Instead he tried to capture an image on a printing plate. "With patience anything can be done," Niepce told Claude, and patience was certainly what he needed. For years, he methodically tried one technique after another,

French inventor Joseph Nicéphore Niepce made the first permanent photographic images.

coating metal plates with various substances. Finally, in 1822, he came upon something that worked: a type of asphalt called bitumen of Judea, which was usually used to surface roads. When exposed to light, the dark bitumen would fade to a slightly lighter color. Even more importantly, the exposed surfaces would turn rock hard, while unexposed surfaces would stay softer. As a result, after an image was projected onto a plate coated with bitumen, the softer, unexposed portions could be washed away, leaving a permanent image in relief. Niepce called these images on asphalt "heliographs," or "sun pictures."

In 1827, in his first attempt to capture a natural scene with his new method, Niepce placed a pewter plate coated with bitumen of Judea inside a camera obscura at his workroom window, exposing it to the view outdoors all day in bright sunlight. Once the unexposed portions were washed away, what remained on the plate was a very faint but recognizable positive view of the buildings that stood outside the window. Remarkably, after having been lost for more than a century, this plate (still bearing its ghostly image) was discovered in a storage trunk in 1952, and it is now part of an important photography collection in Texas.

To look at this plate today — or even a photographic reproduction of it — is like getting a glimpse of the birth of a great art. But in truth, the image is very hard to see, and the technique used to make it was impossibly time consuming. For photography to become practical, some way would have to be found to greatly reduce this exposure time.

Niepce had proven that he had both the patience and the creativity to overcome problems that had stymied many inventors before him. Try as he might, however, he couldn't seem to take the last steps toward making his inventions a commercial success. He needed a partner, preferably one with a stronger business sense. The man he ended up with was a French inventor named Louis Jacques Mandé Daguerre. The two men couldn't have been more different. Niepce was quiet, perhaps shy, cautious in everything he did. Daguerre, on the other hand, was a cheerful, outgoing man who loved attention and publicity.

In 1822 Daguerre had been proclaimed a magician for his invention of the Diorama, a huge multimedia show that was a sensation in Paris. In many ways, the Diorama was an ancestor of the movies: Audiences sat in a large, darkened theater, facing an enormous screen that was as much as forty-five feet high and seventy feet wide. As viewers watched, a series of lights would gradually illuminate the screen from above and below, in front and behind, slowly and dramatically revealing the details of a super-realistic painting to the accompaniment of music and other sound effects.

For example, one scene at first seemed to show only the empty interior of a church in daylight. Then the lights in the theater went down and suddenly

In 1827 Niepce made this ghostly image from the studio of his home in France. It is the world's earliest known photograph.

19

small lights from behind the screen made it seem as if the church interior were being lit by candles. Other lights would suddenly reveal people sitting in the pews, painted but seeming all-too-real. The haunting music of the organ would begin to swell, and the audience, suddenly transported to a midnight mass in a stunningly beautiful church, would gasp.

Daguerre used a camera obscura to help create the Diorama's giant paintings, projecting and tracing the church scene and others, and then using the tracings to produce the most accurate painting possible. But this was laborious, extremely time-consuming work. Wouldn't it be wonderful, Daguerre dreamed, if somehow the painting could be replaced by an image reproduced directly from life?

When he heard that a man named Niepce was working toward a similar goal elsewhere in France, Daguerre wasted no time in contacting the older inventor. In 1827 they met in Paris, where Niepce viewed his first two Dioramas, both of which showed outdoor landscapes. Describing them to his son Isidore, he wrote, "These representations are so real, even in their smallest detail, that one believes that he actually sees rural and primeval nature with all the fascination with which charm of colors and the magic of light and shade endow it."

Daguerre was equally impressed with Niepce's heliographs. Daguerre knew that these faint, faded images were far from the quality he'd need for his Diorama, but he also saw that the achievement was an important one with

Before he met Niepce, Daguerre was best known for his magnificent Dioramas, giant realistic paintings that he would gradually and dramatically reveal to an audience, along with music and special effects. This pair of Diorama images shows a Swiss village before and after its destruction by an avalanche.

great potential. He believed that all it would take was hard work to make photography a reality. The two men became partners in 1829, and indeed Daguerre began to work hard, disappearing into his laboratory for days on end. "He is always at the thought; he cannot sleep at night," his wife complained in a letter to a friend. "I am afraid he is out of his mind."

Daguerre and Niepce both continued to struggle to improve the potential of heliography. Within a year or two, though, Daguerre had given up on using bitumen of Judea and focused on coating paper with light-sensitive silver compounds, as Thomas Wedgwood had done; only Daguerre mixed the silver powder with iodine to increase its sensitivity to light.

In 1837, four years after Niepce's sudden death, Daguerre came up with

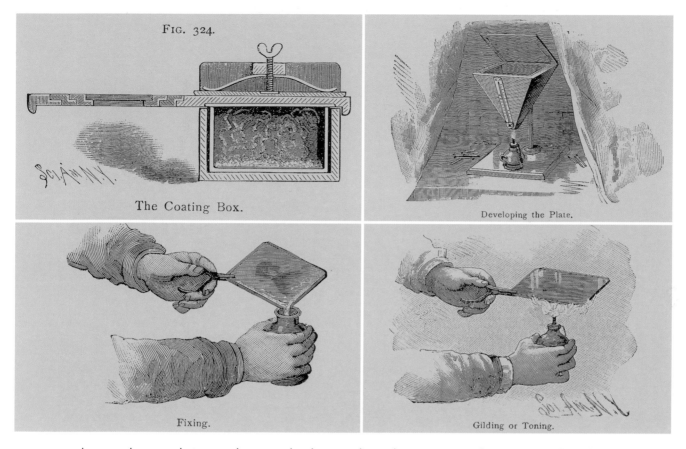

FIG. 324.

The Coating Box.

Developing the Plate.

Fixing.

Gilding or Toning.

a silver-iodine technique that worked. He placed a copper plate, coated with silver and carefully polished, into a box containing iodine vapor. This vapor mixed with the silver coating to form a compound called silver iodide, which is very light sensitive.

Daguerre then placed the sensitized plate inside a camera — still a simple box with a lens, as it had been for centuries — and took a picture. At the beginning, this meant exposing the plate to a brightly lit scene for at least fifteen or twenty minutes. Though this was still a long time by today's standards, it was a vast improvement over the eight hours Niepce had needed to form an image on his bitumen-covered plate.

After the exposure was completed, Daguerre put the plate into a box con-

After being coated in a special "coating box," the plate was inserted into a camera and exposed to light as the daguerreotype was taken. The image captured on the plate was then developed (by exposure to mercury vapor heated over a lamp), fixed (by treatment with the chemical hydrosulphite), rinsed, and dried. It was a slow and difficult process — but better than anything that came before.

taining mercury vapor. The mercury interacted with the specks of silver that had formed where the sun had struck to create large pale spots, which to the eye formed silvery patterns corresponding to the lightest objects in the scene that had been photographed. The dark polished silver of the unexposed portions of the plate, where the sunlight-silver-mercury interaction hadn't taken place, represent the darker areas of the scene. In one more advance, perhaps the most important of all, Daguerre was able to make the image permanent by washing the plate in a salt solution. He then discovered that he could achieve a better result by using a salt compound, sodium thiosulphate (hypo), which dissolved and removed all the unexposed silver iodide, making the plate permanent.

Daguerre, never shy, named his process the daguerreotype, and the name soon caught on. More poetically, others took to calling it "the mirror with a memory."

When Daguerre announced his process in January 1839, the public and press were very enthusiastic. Due to his spectacular Dioramas, Daguerre was already known to be able to work wonders. By inventing his "mirror with a memory," he'd created his greatest trick so far. And this one was no illusion.

Gazing at the first daguerreotypes on display in Paris, people were stunned by the images' clarity and detail. "From today, painting is dead!" the great painter Paul Delaroche supposedly said — and others were just as amazed. Describing a picture of a bridge and wharf along the River Seine in Paris, a writer in an American magazine exclaimed, "[A]ll the minutest indentations and divisions of the ground, of the building, the goods lying on the wharf, even the small stones under the water at the edge of the stream, and the different degrees of transparency given to the water, were all shown with the most incredible accuracy." Photography had come a very long way since Niepce had made his first heliograph twelve years earlier.

Having seen Daguerre's creations, people immediately wanted to take daguerreotypes for themselves. In August 1839, a Paris lecture by Daguerre's associates, followed by the publication of a brochure explaining every step of

the process, sent dozens of hopeful photographers to shops to buy the boxes, lenses, plates, and chemicals necessary to make daguerreotypes. "Everyone wished to copy the view from his window," reported a writer of the time named Gaudin. Each new photographer, he added, "went into ecstasies over chimney tops, he counted again and again roof tiles and chimney bricks, he was astonished to see the very mortar between the bricks — in a word, the technique was so new and seemed so marvelous that even the poorest proof gave him an indescribable joy."

Because of the long exposure time, this 1839 daguerreotype of a busy Paris street looks almost deserted. Anything that moved didn't register. In fact, a man who was having his shoes shined (bottom left) is the only one who stood still long enough to show up in the picture.

While this excitement was taking hold, Daguerre himself quickly lost interest in this public passion, choosing instead to go back to an older form of artistic expression: painting. Almost immediately, though, other inventors began working to improve the process. One, William Henry Fox Talbot, had been working in England on a very different photographic technique of his own since 1833, the year that Joseph Niepce died.

Like Thomas Wedgwood years earlier, Talbot focused on the possibility of capturing images on paper, instead of plates. The idea came to him, he said, as he experimented with projecting images with a camera obscura onto a piece of white paper: "How charming it would be if it were possible to cause these natural images to imprint themselves durably, and remain fixed upon the paper!" he wrote.

Like others with the same charming idea, Talbot went to his laboratory and began to experiment with coating paper with silver compounds, and soon found that it was possible to reproduce a real-life scene projected through the camera obscura. Again like others, he also discovered that the image faded away to nothing if exposed even to weak light. At first Talbot, like Daguerre, preserved his images by bathing them in a strong salt solution. This bath was at least partly effective. No longer was it necessary to view paper photographs by candlelight in a dark room. At the suggestion of the scientist Sir John Herschel, he also began to use sodium thiosulphate (hypo) to make his images permanent.

Talbot called his images "photogenic drawings." Since the paper's light-sensitive coating darkened on exposure to the sun, they were negative images — that is, all the tones were reversed, with the dark parts appearing light, and vice versa. Talbot realized that in order to make his pictures lifelike he had to reverse the tones, and he soon devised a clever, easy way to transform these negative images into positive ones.

He waxed a completed photogenic drawing — turning the paper surrounding the image transparent — then laid it atop another piece of coated, light-sensitive white paper and exposed the whole thing to sunlight. The sunlight came strongly through the lighter portions of the original, turning those portions of the copy underneath dark. Meanwhile, the dark parts of the original blocked the sunlight, leaving those areas of the copy white. This process produced a black-and-white image whose tints corresponded with those in real life. As an added bonus, by using this technique, Talbot found that he could make as many positive images as he wanted by repeating the process.

What Talbot did, in the most basic possible way, was invent the photographic negative and the positive print. Today, we use the same ideas that this British inventor, working on his own, came up with more than one hundred and fifty years ago.

Talbot announced his inventions to the world soon after Daguerre did in 1839.

In the 1830s, William Henry Fox Talbot invented the positive photographic print — photographs on paper, just like the ones we see today.

He renamed his photographic images "calotypes," though for a while the public and press thought of them as "talbotypes." No matter the name, his new process — especially its ability to produce infinite numbers of copies of an image — was a direct threat to the daguerreotype, with its heavy metal plate and single image that could not be reproduced. A lively competition between the two techniques would last for years. Talbot's calotype was never as popular as the daguerreotype, but the negative/positive principle was the basis of modern photographic systems.

3

THROUGH THE CAMERA'S EYE

From the first announcements of their existence in 1839, through about 1860, the daguerreotype and the calotype were the only two systems of photography available but the daguerreotype was far more popular, particularly because by 1843 it made excellent portraits. It seemed as if everyone in Europe and the United States wanted to take pictures or have their pictures taken.

The daguerreotype's success was partly due to the fact that Daguerre quickly made it available to the public, publishing careful, easy-to-follow instructions on building a camera. If you didn't want to build your own, Daguerre's equipment maker, Alphonse Giroux, could do it for you. Either way, becoming a photographer wasn't cheap, of course: A camera, along with an iodizing box for sensitizing exposed plates, a mercury box for making the images visible, a storage box, and supplies of chemicals, cost the equivalent of eighty dollars — quite a sum in 1840.

Giroux's cameras, beautifully crafted of brass and mahogany, were in many ways small versions of the familiar camera obscura. They were constructed of two sliding boxes, a larger one into which a smaller one would slide. The larger box in front contained a small lens that was carefully ground to minimize flaws. The rear box was fitted with a mirror to turn the image right-

Opposite
A typical scene in a daguerreotype studio, reproduced on a daguerreotype. The woman is working at a retouching stand, removing flaws from previous images captured by the photographer.

side up and a small ground-glass screen onto which the image was projected.

The photographer would study the image projected on the screen, moving the camera and adjusting the distance to the subject to compose and focus the shot. Once he was satisfied, he would replace the ground-glass screen with a holder for the photographic plate, slide the copper plate coated with silver iodide into the holder, and then take the picture.

The process of preparing to take a daguerreotype was time consuming, and the camera, plates, and boxes were heavy and awkward to carry around. As a result, most daguerreotype cameras were set up in homes or studios. For many people, it was far too much trouble to bring the camera and equipment into the field in order to photograph scenery.

What daguerreotype cameras could do very well, though — especially as they were improved over the years, and exposure times shrunk — was take por-

THE HARRISON
DAGUERREAN STUDIO,
NO. 411 BROADWAY, NEW-YORK.
(OVER ROE LOCKWOOD'S BOOKSTORE,)

traits. If you had enough money, you could go out and have pictures taken of yourself, family, friends, even pets.

Family portraits allowed you to keep a record of the faces of people who were no longer alive or who lived far away. Before photography, the only images of a relative or friend who had died were contained in the memories of those who knew them, since painted portraits were too costly for most people. Now, for the first time, family portraits guaranteed that even people in generations to come would be able to see what their ancestors had looked like.

By the early 1840s, daguerreotype portrait studios were opening across

After Daguerre's invention was revealed, daguerreotype studios sprung up in Europe and North America, and people lined up to have pictures taken.

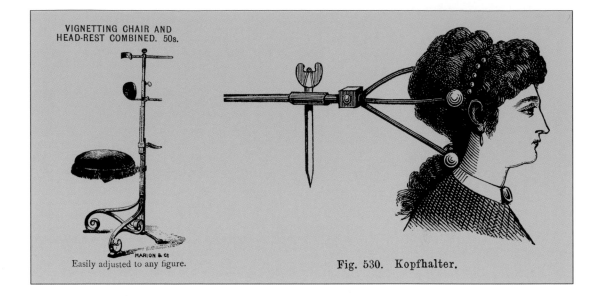

VIGNETTING CHAIR AND
HEAD-REST COMBINED. 50s.

Easily adjusted to any figure.

Fig. 530.   Kopfhalter.

Europe and in the United States. By 1850 there were at least seventy studios in New York City alone. To show off the spectacular new art of photography, these studios were frequently built to resemble palaces or temples, with stained-glass windows, luxurious carpets, and props such as caged birds to liven up the portrait. You could get all this, and a picture of yourself as well, for an affordable two dollars. No wonder daguerreotypes were so popular.

Still, even with advances in lens design and improvements in the light sensitivity of the plates, a person sitting for a daguerreotype portrait had to stay completely still for half a minute or more — a far shorter time than the fifteen minutes required during early daguerreotypes, but still no easy task. The photographer would open the camera's lens (in these early days usually just a lens cap, pivoting metal plate, or piece of dark cloth), and expose the plate for the time it took for the exposure. If you moved at all during this exposure time, your face would appear blurred, and the portrait would be ruined.

Sitting still for so long was difficult. Most studios used a gentle brace to hold the subject's head in place during the exposure. Today, it's easy to see the struggle that went into trying to sit still: The vast majority of daguerreotype

portraits show people looking stiff and unhappy. But there is real beauty in these images as well, in the gorgeous silver tones of the daguerreotype, and even in the faces of the people who sat — people who were participating for the first time in an art that must still have seemed magical to them.

While daguerreotype studios were springing up everywhere, William Henry Fox Talbot continued to improve his calotype process to produce the finest images possible. Probably his biggest breakthrough came in his discovery of the "latent image": a very short exposure left no image on the paper, but if the paper was soaked in a chemical developing agent, a strong image

appeared. Even so, the calotype process never achieved the widespread popularity of the daguerreotype. One reason was that the calotype's image wasn't as brilliant, or as sharp, as the daguerreotype's, so it never became the first choice for portraits.

Still, the calotype had certain advantages over the daguerreotype. Because it used paper instead of silver-coated copper plates, it was less expensive. But most crucial was the fact that a single calotype negative could produce an unlimited number of prints — meaning that, for the first time, photographers could make money selling their images to more than a single person at a time.

The Haystack, from Talbot's *The Pencil of Nature* (1844), the first book to be illustrated with photographs.

Englishman Frederick Scott Archer (c. 1849 self-portrait, *above*) developed the collodion, or "wet-plate" process, which by 1860 would replace both the daguerreotype and Talbot's paper calotype. Archer used the collodion process to make this image of Hadley Church in England.

In the 1840s and 1850s, calotypes provided people in Europe and the United States with their first photographic views of the scenic splendors of distant lands. Even today, these early calotypes of Greek statues, French cathedrals, country lanes, and city scenes in a dozen cities seem to possess the excitement not only of art, but also of discovery.

Between them, the daguerreotype and the calotype created a fervor for photography. In 1844 Talbot published *The Pencil of Nature*, a history of the calotype that was the first book ever to be illustrated with photographs. By the 1850s many books were illustrated with photographs. By the mid-nineteenth century there were also dozens of books on the art and science of photography ranging from how-to manuals to guides to building your own cameras and grinding your own lenses.

At the same time, the number of professional photographers taking portraits in studios or trekking through the wilderness in search of the perfect piece of scenery continued to mushroom. Stores specializing in selling camera equipment sprang up in every city and many towns, and so did the factories supplying them. Museums, galleries, and fairs began showcasing exhibitions of photographs and paying prize money to those who took the finest images. Police departments began using photographs on their Most Wanted posters. It was a remarkable time, as people who just a few years before would have dismissed the whole idea of photography as a magician's trick now found they couldn't live without it.

This widespread enthusiasm for photography was due entirely to the arrival of the daguerreotype and calotype. Yet those two processes would barely survive photography's early boom years. By the 1850s an Englishman called Frederick Scott Archer had invented a system that would be called the "wet-plate," or collodion, process. A glass plate was coated with a sticky, syrupy material known as collodion that had been mixed with a very small quantity of a chemical called ammonium bromide. The plate was then immersed in a bath of silver nitrate forming light-sensitive silver bromide. It was essential to expose and develop the plate when it was still wet — when it dried, it lost sensitivity. The wet plate was placed in the camera, and a picture was taken. After an exposure of between three and twelve seconds depending on lighting conditions, a negative image was produced that was more finely detailed than the calotype and which didn't suffer from the graininess caused by the calotype's paper negative.

Archer was also primarily responsible for an image called an "ambrotype." A developed wet-plate negative was mounted in a case against a black background. This had the effect of apparently reversing the tones of the negative, the white areas becoming dark and the dark areas simply becoming darker. Although not as brilliant as a daguerreotype, the ambrotype was much cheaper to make.

A variation on the ambrotype was the "tintype." A piece of thin steel was

painted black, coated with collodion, and sensitized. The developed picture, usually a portrait, was positive without any further treatment, and had the added advantage of being almost indestructible. Tintypes could be sent through the mail, and millions were produced during the American Civil War to be exchanged by families and troops in the field. Portrait studios started appearing in such unlikely places as butchers and dentists' offices, and it was possible to pose for an ambrotype or tintype and take home a photograph for just a handful of change.

Still, photographers wanting to take pictures outside the studio had to confront the one big drawback of this process: the collodion plate had to be exposed and developed almost immediately after being prepared. This meant that photographers had to carry darkrooms with them, so they would be able to prepare the plate and load the camera without exposing the plate to sunlight. They also had to carry all the chemicals required to coat, sensitize, develop, and fix the plate.

As a result, it was common to see professional photographers carrying portable darkrooms (actually, easily erected tents) on their backs. Others chose even more elaborate solutions. Mathew Brady, an award-winning daguerreotypist who was one of the first to abandon that technique for the collodion process, took a wagon (dubbed the "What Is It" wagon) onto the battlefields of the Civil War. There he employed a staff of twenty photographers, who sent back graphic and horrifying visual accounts of the tolls of war. Meanwhile, other pioneering photographers built and rode specially designed railroad cars to take the first photographs of the American West.

Such portable darkrooms soon became an expected sight in even the most remote corners of the United States and Europe, and across the world. As a

Mathew Brady took his first portrait of President Abraham Lincoln on February 27, 1861. Thanks to the wide-spread distribution of Brady's photographs, Lincoln's striking face soon became familiar all across the United States.

result, the public finally got to see the differences between the faces of people in distant countries and their own; how the landscapes of tropical regions differed from their homelands; and what important local and foreign people (from Abraham Lincoln to Queen Victoria) really looked like.

To make their jobs a little easier, photographers kept tinkering with their cameras, trying to make the bulky device they'd used while taking daguerreotypes in the studio a more portable camera for fieldwork. One innovative idea, introduced around 1860, was the folding bellows camera, in which nearly everything was collapsible: The lens could be pushed into the body of the camera, and the box folded in on itself, making a package that was relatively easy to carry.

An even more significant advance — and one that photographers had been hoping would come about since the collodion process was invented in

the early 1850s — finally arrived in the late 1870s, when the first photographic dry-plate process was invented. A glass plate coated with dried gelatin, an almost colorless protein obtained by boiling animal hooves and bones, was then coated with a light-sensitive emulsion and could be used at any time. Photographers carried the individual dry plates with them, took pictures easily when and where they liked, and then waited until returning home to develop and print the pictures.

In an 1860 magazine article, scientist and photographer John Herschel had dreamed of "the possibility of taking a photograph, as it were, by a snap-shot — of securing a picture in a tenth of a second of time." Now, in 1878, this dream had become a reality, and the era of the snapshot had begun.

For the first time, photographers began recording the images of everyday

Left
Advances in camera design and photographic processing allowed photographers to travel to remote regions, set up "photographic camps," and send back pictures.

Right
Photographs for sale! George E. Mellen, of Gunnison, Colorado, was the proprietor of this movable photograph store.

life: busy marketplace scenes, kids playing in the street, people swimming in the surf, the crowds at a ball game. A public that had barely gotten used to the stiff poses in daguerreotypes was amazed to see these lively scenes reproduced on a piece of paper.

Remarkably, it now became possible to freeze movements from life that were too quick to see with the eye alone — to truly see how people and animals looked as they moved. And thanks to some dedicated photographers, especially a man named Eadweard Muybridge, the public soon learned that the naked eye was not an accurate judge of many of the movements we take for granted.

Muybridge aligned a dozen or more specially designed high-speed cameras and photographed people, horses, camels, or other animals as they trotted, ran, or jumped past. The results were so strange and spectacular —

Have camera, will travel. Smaller cameras meant the birth of the travel photograph, such as this picture of the Taj Mahal taken by John Murray in the 1850s.

Photography allowed people to see exotic images such as the Colossus of Ramses II at Abu Simbel, Egypt, taken by Maxime du Camp in 1852.

Muybridge was the first to show, for example, that all four of a horse's feet leave the ground as it trots — that at first many people refused to believe what his photographs showed. The London *Globe* was typically annoyed, complaining that when enjoying a painting of a horse race, lovers of art did not need "Mr. Muybridge to tell us that no horses ever strode in the fashion shown in the picture. It may indeed be fairly contended," the newspaper huffed, "that the incorrect position (according to science) is the correct position (according to art)."

Such controversies, along with the flood of newly published and exhibited photographs that gelatin dry plates made possible, spurred yet another surge in public interest in photography. In response, manufacturers began producing a startling array of new cameras. The first practical movie camera was made in the early 1890s using a modified form of film designed by George Eastman. These cameras used film perforated on both edges and mounted on sprockets that would move past the lens to take a series of photographs in rapid succession. When projected onto a screen, the resulting images seemed to move. Another important advance was the arrival of smaller handheld cameras to replace the bulky old models that stood on tripods or other stands.

The invention of the gelatin dry plate opened up a whole new world of camera design. The wet-plate process, with its messy corrosive chemicals, required manufacturers to keep their designs simple. With the invention of the dry plate, it was possible to make a variety of unusual designs. Since the ground-glass screen long used for focusing and composing the image could not be shrunk, it was replaced or augmented by a viewfinder (a small lens attached to the outside of the camera, through which the photographer could see the area to be photographed before pushing the button) and a distance scale (a series of markings on the main lens telling the photographer how to adjust the lens depending on the distance from the subject). The first true shutters, capable of uncovering and then covering the lens in a fraction of a second, were also added. They were a necessity, given the short new exposure times brought

Opposite
Eadweard Muybridge was the first to take stop-action photographs, in which movements — even familiar ones — are broken down and begin to seem unfamiliar. Even after seeing these photographs, many people refused to believe that trotting horses actually pick all four legs up off the ground at the same time.

about by the light sensitivity of the gelatin dry plates. Powered by springs or rubber bands, the first shutters were usually made up of small metal disks or plates that would slide quickly over the lens, leaving the film exposed for a length of time determined by the photographer.

In the early 1880s, the most popular smaller cameras were called "detective cameras." They were designed to allow you to "play detective," taking photographs of people without their knowledge. To this end, detective cameras came disguised as bags, hats (you took the picture by pulling a string attached to the hat brim), the handles of walking sticks, gift boxes, pistols, watches, and other familiar objects.

Today, these nineteenth-century spy cameras look a lot like . . . well, like cameras trying to disguise themselves as something else. But at the time the disguises were often successful, and the public got its first unwelcome taste of

Early on, photography developed into an art form rivaling painting, as is shown by this 1865 photograph entitled *May Day*, by Julia Margaret Cameron *(left)*, and Clarence H. White's *Ring Toss* (1899, *right*).

being photographed candidly. Articles and drawings of the time make it clear that, however much fun it was to sneak around with a detective camera, it was far less enjoyable to be the subject of such a photograph.

What was most important about the detective-camera fad was that it pushed camera manufacturers to design smaller and smaller cameras. The result was a portable unit shaped like an oblong box, with a viewfinder, focusing scale, lens, shutter, and a handle or carrying strap. The compact camera was just big enough to hold the glass plates that were now available in a number of sizes. Amateurs typically used 4 by 5 or 5 by 7 inch plates. The dry plate could be loaded by the photographer just before he took the picture.

The pieces were falling in place for photography to become massively popular, but there were still three hurdles ahead: As much as the camera had shrunk, it would have to become even smaller. The need to use a separate coated glass

Left
By the 1890s, it seemed that everyone wanted to be a photographer.

Right
Spy cameras — often concealed inside everyday objects like this cravat — allowed people to take the first candid photographs.

47

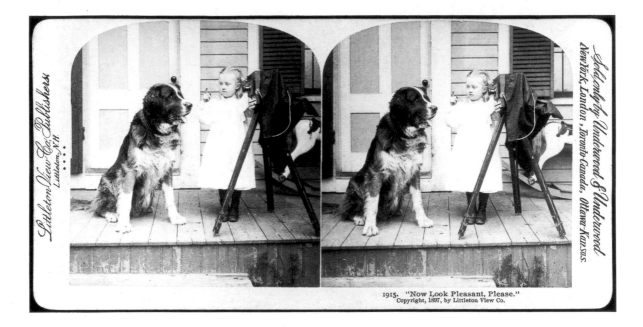

Stereoscopic photographs, such as this whimsical image of a girl pretending to photograph a large dog, were popular in the mid- to late nineteenth century. The double photograph was inserted into a handheld viewer called a stereopticon to create a more lifelike, three-dimensional image.

plate for each picture was also a problem. Even though the gelatin dry-plate process made photography truly portable, the plates themselves were still heavy, fragile, and awkward to use. After each exposure, you still had to wrestle the plate out of the camera, stash it in a safe place, and slide another one in. What's more, you then had to go home and develop and print all the images. There were no one-hour photo shops, no photo-processing laboratories. Just as Talbot and other photography pioneers had done, you had to build your own darkroom, stock the right chemicals, and know how to use them.

No matter how much they would have loved to take pictures, most people just weren't willing or able to take on all the chores and expense involved with photography. Someone was going to have to come up with something that was easier to use than glass plates and make the process of taking, developing, and printing a photograph so simple that there would be no reason not to take up photography as a hobby.

The job fell to a brilliant man named George Eastman, who finally made the camera easily available to the world.

THE DEVELOPMENT OF THE CAMERA

Since its invention some 175 years ago, the function of the camera has changed very little; we still use it to record visual images of the world around us. The camera still consists of a lens — which reduces the image of a full-sized subject — and it still records the reduced image, whether on film, paper, or electronically. What has changed is the precision of the lenses, the speed of the shutters, the sensitivity of the film, and most dramatically, the "body" of the camera. The **camera obscura** appeared in the middle of the 16th century. It was made in several forms, but the most common was a simple box fitted with a lens at one end and a sketching surface at the other.

Camera obscura

1839: The Giroux Daguerreotype Camera was the first camera made for sale to the public. It made an image 6 1/2 by 8 1/2 inches. There was no shutter, just a simple rotating slide mechanism in front of the lens. The photographer focused the camera by sliding the slightly smaller rear box in and out of the larger box. The low sensitivity of the plates and the slow lens meant that only subjects that did not move could be photographed.

1841: The Voigtlander Daguerreotype Camera was the first camera to be fitted with the Petzval portrait lens. The speed of this lens enabled photographers to make portraits of people. Pictures from this camera were circular and measured just 3 7/10 inches in diameter. It was also the first all-metal camera sold to the public.

1851: The Lewis Daguerreotype Camera, the first bellows-style camera to be produced in quantity, came in several sizes, but the most common was the so-called quarter-plate size, which made pictures measuring 3 1/4 by 4 1/4 inches. The adjustable bellows replaced the sliding boxes of the earlier Daguerreotype. For years it was the favorite camera of professional photographers and serious amateurs.

Giroux daguerreotype

1856: The Kinnear Folding Wet-Plate Camera was the first to be fitted with a tapered folding bellows, which reduced the camera's size considerably. Each fold of the bellows fit into the previous one, creating a general system that is still in use today. The Kinnear camera made 10 1/2- by 12 1/2-inch plates.

1874: The Scenographe Dry-Plate Camera could fit into a large pocket, but despite its small size, it made full 6 1/2- by 8 1/2-inch images. Dry plates were becoming available in limited quantities when this camera was introduced. The camera had no shutter — just a lens cap that was removed to make the exposure.

Color Film

Color film is a very complex product. It is represented here in simplified form. In addition to the base and numerous layers that control **color balance**, there are three layers that are each sensitive to one of the primary photographic colors: **red**, **green**, or **blue**. The colors that make up the subject being photographed are recorded in the appropriate layers of film. Either a color negative or a positive slide is produced, depending on the type of film used.

Red, green, and blue light is recorded on the corresponding layers of the color film. To produce white, all of the layers are exposed. Once the image is recorded on film, a complicated developing process transforms it into a color print. The color print paper is similar to the film because it, too, has layers that respond to different colors.

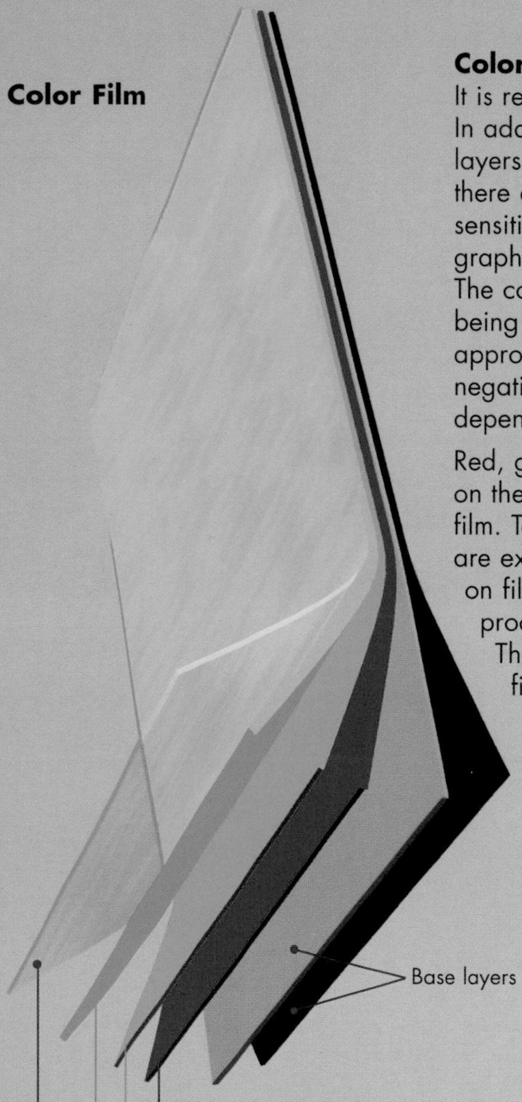

Base layers

Blue-sensitive layer

Green-sensitive layer

Red-sensitive layer

Color balance layer

Kinnear folding wet-plate

Kodak

1888: The Kodak Camera made it possible for just about anyone to take pictures. It was the first camera made for the unskilled amateur "snapshot" photographer. Each camera came loaded with enough film for one hundred 2 1/2-inch circular photographs. When it was used up, the entire camera was returned to the factory where the pictures were developed and the camera was reloaded with fresh film. The introduction of the Bulls Eye Box Camera by the Boston Camera Company in 1892 made this even easier. It used film that could be loaded and unloaded in subdued light and did not require returning the camera to the factory or to the darkroom. The Bulls Eye Box made 3 1/2-inch square pictures.

1900: The Brownie Camera was, in its day, the least expensive camera capable of taking an adequate picture; it cost just $1. Each picture was 2 1/2 inches square. There were six exposures on a roll of film, which cost 10 cents. The first in a long line of cheap, easy-to-operate Kodak cameras, it was intended for children but soon caught on with amateur photographers of all ages, and millions were sold.

1925: The Leica Camera was the first successful camera to use 35-millimeter film. It made 24- by 36-millimeter images on strips of movie film. The Leica was designed by Oskar Barnack, who worked for the German microscope manufacturer E. Leitz. The name came from the words "Leitz" and "camera." An instant success, it sparked interest in miniature photography.

1934: The Kodak Baby Brownie made use of an industrial plastic called Bakelite. It made 1 5/8 inch- by 2 1/2-inch pictures on 127 roll film. The use of Bakelite lowered production costs considerably, so that the camera's price was just $1 — the same as the original Brownie more than thirty years earlier.

1883: The Stebbing Roll Film Camera, the first to use only roll film (paper coated with photographic chemicals and wound on a roll), started a new era in photography. The picture size was 2 1/4 by 2 9/10 inches. Most of the cameras at the time were designed for dry plates but could be fitted with accessory roll film holders.

1939: The Super Kodak 620 was the first camera to offer completely automatic exposure control. The photographer selected a shutter speed, and a delicate mechanism powered by sunlight adjusted the lens opening. The brighter the sun, the smaller the opening, and vice versa. It made images 2 1/4 by 3 1/4 inches on 620 roll film.

RECORDING AN IMAGE

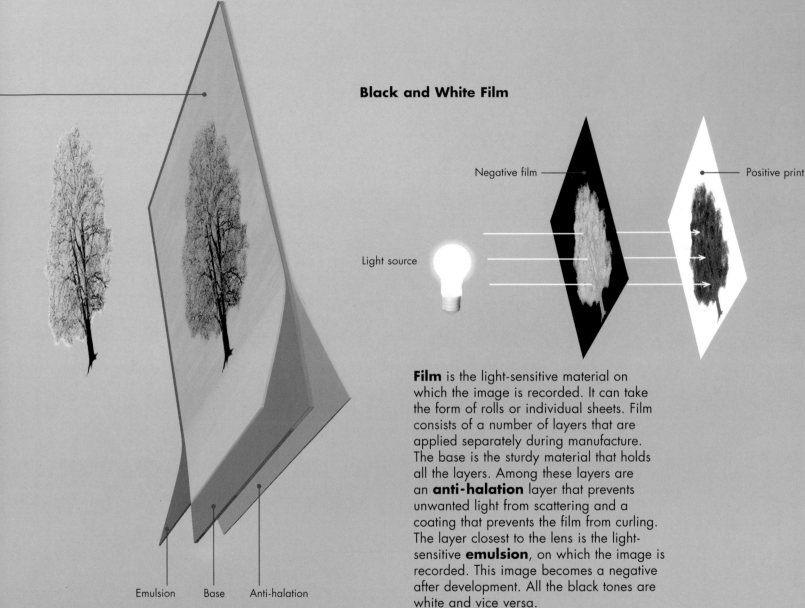

Black and White Film

Emulsion   Base   Anti-halation

Light source

Negative film

Positive print

Film is the light-sensitive material on which the image is recorded. It can take the form of rolls or individual sheets. Film consists of a number of layers that are applied separately during manufacture. The base is the sturdy material that holds all the layers. Among these layers are an **anti-halation** layer that prevents unwanted light from scattering and a coating that prevents the film from curling. The layer closest to the lens is the light-sensitive **emulsion**, on which the image is recorded. This image becomes a negative after development. All the black tones are white and vice versa.

The **positive print** — the photograph — is made by passing light through the negative and exposing the image onto photographic paper. The darkest areas on the negative hold back light and produce the lightest areas on the print; light areas on the negative let in more light and produce dark areas on the print.

1948: The Polaroid 95 Camera was the world's first **instant camera**. Its 3 1/4- by 4 1/4-inch pictures were taken on a special picture roll that contained all the chemicals needed to process the film inside the camera. The photographer pulled the film and paper between two stainless steel rollers. This caused a packet of chemicals mounted next to each photograph to open and started a 60-second developing process. The finished picture was simply removed from the back of the camera. In 1972, the Polaroid Corporation introduced an instant camera called the SX70. It automatically ejected full color pictures that developed in broad daylight.

Instant camera

1949: The Contax S Camera was the first modern **single-lens reflex camera**. Fitted with a viewing prism, it could be held comfortably at eye level. (Previous reflex cameras were held at waist level, and the photographer looked down into a viewing surface.) It used standard 35-millimeter film cassettes and made 24- by 36-millimeter images. With tens of millions sold, the 35-millimeter single-lens reflex is the most popular camera among professionals and serious amateurs.

Single-lens reflex

1986: The first **Single-Use Camera** was made by Fuji and was factory-loaded with 24 exposures on 35-millimeter film. Eastman Kodak followed shortly with its own version. Precision injection molded plastics, quality plastic lenses, and greatly improved color negative films made these cameras possible. Perhaps one-third of the more than 23 billion snapshots taken all over world each year are made with them.

Single-use

1990: The Digital Camera marks another revolution in photography — the use of computers. Instead of film, a digital camera uses a charge-coupled device (CCD) that is light sensitive. It records an image and stores it on a computer chip, memory card or a regular floppy disc. This electronic information is transferred from the CCD to a computer and sometimes directly to a printer. The Sony Mavica was the first digital camera; other makers of cameras and electronics, such as Nikon, Canon, and JVC, have produced their own versions.

Leica

Digital camera

THE PARTS OF A CAMERA

All cameras consist of a light-proof box with a lens at one end and a light-sensitized material at the other end. A simple fixed-focus camera does not require focusing, while a more complicated instrument may use a **bellows** or other system to move the lens and sharpen the image.

The **lens** may consist of a very simple single element or a combination of several elements that allow for more complex photography.

The **shutter** is a mechanical device that opens and shuts very quickly and lets in just enough light to freeze a moving image on the film. The time the shutter is open usually lasts less than 1/100th of a second, but it can be as little as 1/12,000th of a second. A shutter can be positioned at the lens or at the film surface.

The **aperture** lets the photographer control the amount of light that reaches the film, depending on the available light surrounding the subject. When open, it allows the maximum amount of light through. It can be closed if the subject is too bright or opened if the subject is too dark. It is the combination of shutter speed and opening of the aperture that assures that the proper amount of light reaches the film.

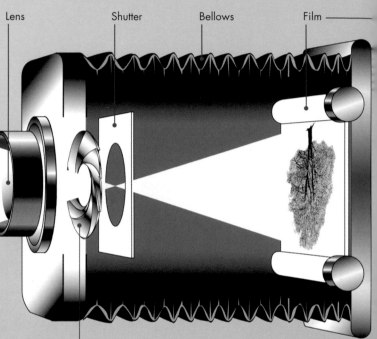

Lens   Shutter   Bellows   Film

Aperture

The shutter and the aperture work together to allow enough light to reach the film. When a subject is moving the shutter opens and closes quickly to catch the image. When a subject is stationary the shutter can be open longer and the aperture can be closed more.

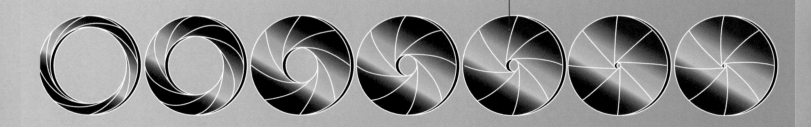

In order to operate this
elaborate late nineteenth-
century twin-lens camera,
the photographer had to
have some knowledge of
photographic procedures.

4
CAMERAS FOR EVERYONE

Born in 1854 in Waterville, New York, George Eastman was a hard worker from the time he was a child, saving his money with the goal of doing something important (and profitable) with his life. By 1877, when he was just twenty-three and working as a bank clerk, he'd already saved $3,000, a remarkable amount for the time.

Fascinated by photography, Eastman set up a business manufacturing photographic plates in Rochester, New York. Not knowing whether his new venture would be a success, he continued working at the bank. The casual nature of his start-up company — but also his brilliant design instincts — can be seen in his design of a container for the emulsion that would be spread on the photographic plates. "A big cask to hold 120 [gallons] in the corner of the washroom, cased in sawdust to hold water and ice, pipe through the floor down into the cellar where the ice water can be drawn directly into the jars," he wrote. "The emulsion is to be stirred by machinery so that $^3/_4$ of the work and all of the sloppiness will be done away with."

The timing of Eastman's entry into the glass-plate business couldn't have been better. The Eastman Dry Plate Company was an immediate success in the early 1880s, catering to the booming market for detective and other cameras.

Opposite
George Eastman was determined to make a success of himself from an early age. He left school when he was only fourteen and immediately got to work on a variety of ambitious projects. This photograph was taken in 1868, when Eastman was fourteen.

PORTABLE PHOTOGRAPHIC APPARATUS.

As far as they'd come, cameras still left a lot to be desired in terms of portability. By 1874, when the engraving at *left* was made, a photographer using the wet-collodion process carried his apparatus on his back. At *right*, George Eastman was the brunt of a joke on the same subject in a 1923 Rochester newspaper.

But Eastman himself was not satisfied. As many people as there were taking pictures, he saw that there were millions of others in the United States and across the world who were not, and he wanted to convince them to start.

First, Eastman decided to try to figure out a way to replace the heavy and fragile glass plates that made carrying the equipment such a chore. He began to experiment with the idea of a paper negative, coating different kinds of paper with the dry gelatin emulsion currently used in most photographic plates. If he succeeded, the result would be a far less bulky negative, which then could be used to print as many positive images as the photographer desired.

In the early 1880s, Eastman introduced his first coated paper — cut into sheets the same size as the glass plates it was replacing — but found the public response disappointing. It was clear that improvements were necessary, so Eastman went back to the laboratory.

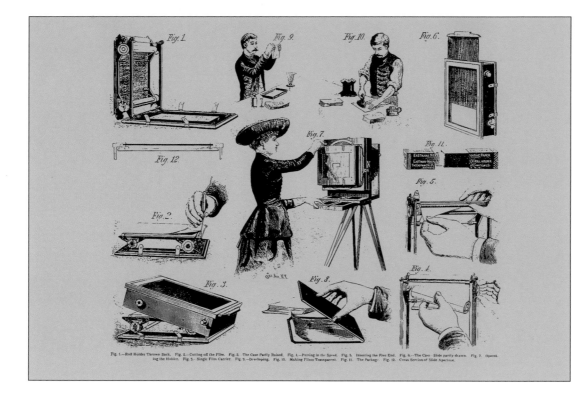

His next invention was one of the most important in the history of the camera. Eastman created an emulsion-coated paper that was flexible enough to be wound into a roll. Each roll had enough paper for twenty-four or more exposures. Working with camera maker William H. Walker, Eastman also designed a special rollholder that fit into almost any camera. After each exposure, the photographer would wind the paper by turning a key and be immediately ready to take another photograph, without having to remove a glass plate or even a sheet of paper and insert another.

The first rolls came to market in 1885, and though they sold well, Eastman still wasn't satisfied. Eastman himself knew that the photographic process had to be made easier still — a truly popular camera would have to be completely foolproof and easy to use.

Eastman enlisted the help of Frank Brownell, an independent camera maker

Among his many break-throughs, George Eastman produced coated film that could be mounted on a roller. This *Scientific American* illustration showed how it was prepared.

who made Eastman's rollholders. The team of Eastman, Brownell, and their coworkers created a new box camera, just six and a half inches long, three and three-quarter inches high, and three and a quarter inches wide. This was one of the most compact cameras yet invented. It could be held in one hand or slipped into a pocket. You could take it anywhere.

What's more, each of these new cameras held enough paper roll film to make one hundred exposures before reloading. All the user had to do was take a picture, advance the film, and tug on a small string that hung from the camera. Or, as the manual put it: "1. Pull the cord. 2. Turn the key. 3. Press the button." With his new camera, he claimed, photography could be done "without preliminary study, without a darkroom and without chemicals."

This may have been Eastman's greatest stroke of genius: Photographers didn't have to worry about ruining their vacation pictures during processing, because they never touched the film at all. When the camera's owner had finished taking one hundred pictures, he or she would send the whole camera back to Eastman's factory. Here the film would be removed, a new roll would be inserted, and the pictures processed and mounted on individual cards. The entire package would then be mailed back to the owner. In this way, George Eastman founded the photofinishing industry. Today this is a multibillion dollar industry functioning in virtually every country in the world.

This photograph of the first Kodak camera, made in 1888, shows the back of the camera removed to reveal where the 2½-inch-wide roll film fit.

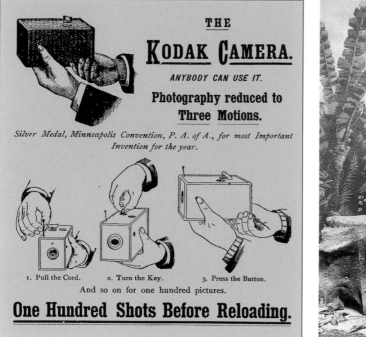

With the eye for business that characterized his career, Eastman came up with a catchy name for his new camera: the Kodak. (He wanted a name that was easy to say, to remember, and to pronounce in any language, and that began with the letter "K," which he thought would draw attention particularly well.) He advertised it with an equally catchy phrase: "You press the button, we do the rest."

The first Kodak hit the market in 1888, and with this product Eastman finally achieved the success he was looking for. During the first year alone, his company sold more than 13,000 Kodaks, a huge number at the time. Further improvements, leading to the introduction of the first modern-style transparent film, only cemented the company's success.

The first Kodak cost $25.00, a substantial sum of money in 1888 when a good weekly factory wage was about $8.00. During the last decade of the nineteenth century, George Eastman's main effort was to develop a less expen-

Left
Early ads emphasized the ease of use and portability of Kodak cameras.

Right
An amateur photographer uses an early factory-loaded Kodak camera circa 1890–92. Eastman's innovations would make it possible for novices to take photographs.

Make pictures 2¼ x 2¼ inches. Load in Daylight with our six exposure film cartridges and are so simple they can be easily

Operated by Any School Boy or Girl.

Fitted with fine Meniscus lenses and our improved rotary shutters for snap shots or time exposures. Strongly made, covered with imitation leather, have nickeled fittings and produce the best results.

Brownie Camera, for 2¼ x 2¼ pictures, . . $1.00
Transparent-Film Cartridge, 6 exposures, 2¼ x 2¼, .15
Brownie Developing and Printing Outfit, . .75

The Brownie Book, a dainty, tiny pamphlet containing fifteen of the prize winning pictures from the Brownie Camera Club Contest, free at any Kodak dealer's or by mail.

EASTMAN KODAK CO.
Rochester, N. Y.

So simple even a child can do it: This was the message of ads for the inexpensive Brownie, both in France and the United States.

sive camera and to reduce costs by devising a method of daylight loading, which could be accomplished by the camera's owner, so that the entire camera did not have to be returned to the factory to be reloaded. Around 1894, Eastman purchased the patent rights to a system of daylight loading that is still used today, more than a century later. In this system, the film was rolled with a sheet of opaque paper printed with numbers indicating each frame to be exposed. These numbers could be read through a little red window in the back of the camera. After taking each picture you simply wound the film onto the next number. When the roll was completed, the photographer could remove it from the camera in regular daylight (though the photographer was cautioned to avoid exposure to strong direct sunlight) and replace it with a fresh roll of film. The finished roll could then be sent to Kodak to be developed and printed.

In 1895, Eastman introduced the Pocket Kodak. This very compact camera was the first completely designed by Eastman Kodak to use spools of daylight

loading film. At $5.00, it was the most affordable Kodak yet.

One of the most important events in the history of snapshot photography was Eastman's introduction of the Brownie camera, designed by Frank Brownell, which retailed for just $1.00. The Brownie used the daylight loading system popularized by Eastman. More than 100,000 were sold in 1900, its first year. The Brownie, which had been intended for the children's market, was quickly embraced by all age groups and became an American classic. Brownie box cameras were still made after the Second World War. Less than a century after the first inventors had begun the struggle to capture "fairy images" on paper or glass, George Eastman made the camera a part of our everyday life.

The extraordinary popularity of Kodak cameras set countless camera designers and manufacturers on a search for other advances in camera design. Perhaps the most important of all was the introduction of the Graflex, a single-lens reflex camera, in 1898. Although it was not the first camera of this type,

The Kodak Brownie, introduced in 1900, cost only $1.00 and used roll film that cost just 15 cents for a six-exposure roll. The design of the packaging made it clear that no special talents were needed to use the camera.

the Graflex was both a first-rate design and extremely sturdy. It soon became the camera of choice for many professional and serious amateur photographers. Today, more than a century later, single-reflex cameras are still the first choice for professional photographers, and for many amateurs as well.

What the single-lens reflex camera does is allow you to see the photograph's exact subject up until the moment you take a picture. You are, in fact, viewing exactly what the camera's lens sees when it takes the picture. The way this works is simple: A mirror is placed between the lens and the film, which reflects the image up onto a small glass screen at the top of the camera. Then, at the moment you press the button to take a photograph, the mirror swings up and out of the way. This allows the image you are photographing to fall on the film instead of the mirror, exposing the film and capturing the image.

Another innovation was the development of the flash. Almost as soon as cameras became widely available, inventors began seeking a way to photograph at night or indoors. It wasn't always possible to use lamps or lightbulbs to illuminate an entire scene brightly enough so that it would register on film. The inventors were looking for a light that would briefly illuminate the subject at the same moment as the picture was taken.

As early as 1860, photographers began to use magnesium powder or a mixture of magnesium and other chemicals to create a very bright and relatively brief flash. By early in the twentieth century this product had become somewhat refined and could be placed in a specially designed pan and ignited as soon as the camera's shutter was opened. The camera had to be mounted on a tripod since the photographer required both hands to manipulate the flash system and the camera's shutter. After the flash, the shutter was

The huge popularity of Kodak cameras set the scene for more camera innovations, including, in 1898, the Graflex, a single-lens reflex camera. With a mirror that reflects the image onto the film, this design incorporated a principle used in the camera obscura.

closed. Flashpowder certainly cast a bright light, but it was smelly, smoky, and extremely unstable, and it often exploded. Photographers lost hands, arms, and even their lives trying to take pictures. Not until 1930 was the first true flashbulb introduced, allowing cameras to safely record images that previously had been beyond their capabilities.

Early in the 1930s the first synchronized flash systems became available. An electric contact in the shutter closed a fraction of a second after the shutter was released. The flashbulb was ignited by a simple circuit powered by flashlight batteries. The photographer, now freed from the need to ignite the flash manually, could hand-hold the camera. The invention of flashbulbs opened up many new opportunities for both professional and amateur photographers.

While manufacturers were seeking to improve camera design, chemists in research laboratories were working towards producing faster and finer-grain films. A faster film required less light to take a picture, and with a finer-grain film it was possible to reduce the negative size and still make a sharp enlarged positive print. Improved films would have a profound effect on camera design.

From early in the 1900s, camera designers had been intrigued by the possibility of using strips of motion-picture film, 35 millimeters wide and perforated on both sides, in still-picture cameras. Several cameras were made and marketed that used 35-millimeter motion-picture film, but they had only limited success. Then, in 1914, German inventor Oskar Barnack made the prototype of a very compact camera that used 35-millimeter film. His employer, Ernst Leitz, was a manufacturer of high-quality microscopes, but the German company was interested in pursuing Barnack's invention. Because of the interruption caused by the First World War, Leitz was unable to make a production version of Barnack's camera until 1925. They called their new camera the Leica, a combination of the words Leitz and camera.

As film and cameras developed, so did flash-bulbs, which made it possible to shoot scenes in areas of limited light. General Electric's largest flashbulb (nine inches high) was made in 1938, and the smallest (only one inch high) in 1975.

The Leica I was small enough to fit in a jacket pocket. It could be loaded with a cassette containing enough film for forty pictures, and the shutter could provide exposures between 1/25th and 1/500th of a second. Even more importantly, a single quick turn of a knob would both advance the film and prepare for the next shot — making the Leica a perfect tool for professional news photographers and anyone else who wanted to take a series of photographs in a quick sequence.

Although some photographers considered the little Leica a "toy," it eventually caught on and became extremely popular. Its success led a number of other manufacturers to build cameras that used 35-millimeter film. Today, eighty years after Oskar Barnack designed the first prototype for the Leica, 35-millimeter film continues to be an important product used extensively by both amateur and professional photographers.

As the use of 35-millimeter film grew, so did the demand for convenient and accurate color film. By the late nineteenth century, inventors were building cameras that were capable of dividing light into three colors — red, green, and blue — and making three separate negatives. These negatives were projected onto three special pieces of film, dyed and then transferred in sequence to a piece of treated paper. The resulting color image was frequently very beautiful, but extremely difficult to make. This technique was used only by a limited number of professional photographers. It was simply too complicated and

Oskar Barnack (*left*) invented the first practical still camera that could use 35-millimeter film. Manufactured by the German company Ernst Leitz, the Leica came on the market in the 1920s. It became the perfect tool for news photographers.

required too much specialized equipment.

Only in the mid-1930s, with the arrival of 35-millimeter Kodachrome film, did true color photography become available to anyone who wanted it. These and other early color films, designed for the production of color slides, used what was called an "integral tripack" emulsion. This meant that the coating on the film contained three separate layers, each of which was sensitive to either red, green, or blue light. The layers also contained dyes and other chemicals that allowed a single photograph to contain all the colors of nature.

Eh' die Blätter fallen

rüsten Sie Ihre Leica für Agfacolor aus; denn
im Herbst hat die Natur die größte Farbenpracht

ERNST LEITZ WETZLAR

Color film became popular almost immediately. A color negative film called Kodacolor was developed by Eastman Kodak in 1942 but did not become available to the consumer until after the Second World War. This product was designed expressly for the easy and inexpensive creation of color prints made by automatic printing machines. By the 1960s color film had become more popular than black-and-white, a dominance that is unlikely ever to change.

While 35-millimeter color film was taking the world by storm, at least one brilliant young inventor was looking in an entirely different direction. His name was Edwin H. Land (1909–91), and by the time he was a teenager attending Harvard College, he had become fascinated by light and what could be done with it.

During a visit to New York City, where he felt overwhelmed by the glaring neon and street lights, Land decided to invent a filter to eliminate that problem. He knew the glare was caused by random vibrations of light waves, and that

In the fall of 1933, this early version of color 35-millimeter photography was promoted as being able to capture the vivid hues of autumn foliage. To create the colors, tinted filters were mounted on the camera lens.

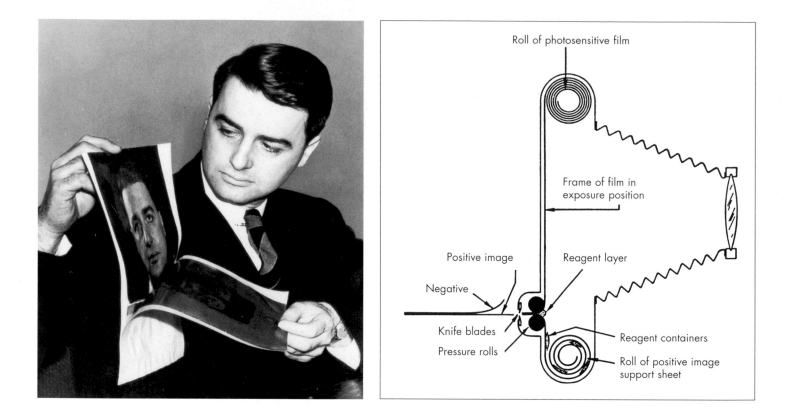

Roll of photosensitive film

Frame of film in exposure position

Positive image

Reagent layer

Negative

Knife blades

Pressure rolls

Reagent containers

Roll of positive image support sheet

special filters might be able to polarize them — to control their vibrations.

At first the laboratories at Harvard wanted nothing to do with this young man and his wild plans. Land solved this problem by breaking into the labs at night, when no one was there, and working till morning. The result: By 1932, Land had designed a plastic sheet containing thousands of tiny crystals of a substance known as herapathite. Light passing through the crystals would be polarized, emerging glare-free.

Although the polarizing filter never gained the wide popularity Land hoped for (the American auto industry thought about requiring such filters on all car headlights, but decided the idea was too expensive), his first invention confirmed Land's fascination with the properties of light. It was only a small step for him to become interested in photography, an art form that depended so heavily on light, and to try to design a better camera.

But Land was unwilling to make only small improvements on earlier technologies. As the story goes, his three-year-old daughter asked him why she had to wait so long to see a picture after it had been taken. Land had no immediate answer to her question, but, as he told *Life* Magazine in 1972, it didn't take him long to come up with one. "Within an hour the camera, the film and the physical chemistry became so clear that with a great sense of excitement I hurried to the place where a friend was staying, to describe to him in detail a dry camera which would give a picture immediately after exposure." His experience with polar-

izing filters and tiny crystals, he added, was invaluable in helping him come up with his revolutionary camera design.

The result of Edwin Land's inspiration was the Model 95 Polaroid Land camera, announced in 1947 and first marketed in 1948. This remarkable camera — and all Polaroid cameras that have followed — in effect place the entire darkroom and processing laboratory within the camera. After the picture was taken, the film was pushed between two rollers. These rollers would break a packet containing processing chemicals and spread them over the exposed film, which would then be developed within a minute or so. While the Polaroid cameras have never completely replaced traditional cameras (the images are inferior, and the lack of a usable negative makes reproductions difficult), it was still amazing that, little more than a century after the arrival of the daguerreotype, truly "instant" photography had finally arrived.

The Model 100 series were the first commercially available cameras to employ an electronic shutter. This feature allows the camera to adjust automatically to the amount of available light.

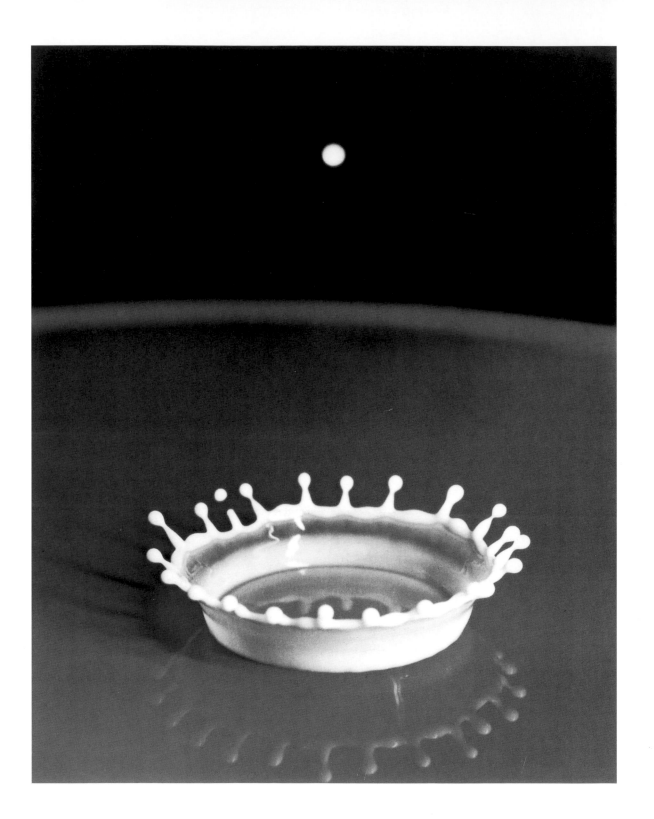

5

IMAGES OF THE FUTURE

In the twentieth century, the camera's booming popularity led manufacturers to continue to improve camera design and extend photography's capabilities ever further.

Since Eadweard Muybridge's photographs of people walking and horses trotting showed that our eyes often don't accurately see what's in front of them, photographers have been fascinated with the idea of freezing movements that are too fast for the eye to see. Although there are now electro-mechanical shutters capable of speeds as fast as 1/14,000th of a second, they still aren't fast enough to freeze such motions as a bird's wings in flight, the shape of the splash after a stone hits the surface of a puddle, or what happens to a bullet at the instant that it strikes a block of steel.

In the 1930s, Harold Edgerton tried a new way of freezing motion for photographs. Instead of working on improving the shutter, he designed the strobe light: a lamp that sends out an intense flash of light for the merest fraction of a second. When a high-speed strobe light is used with a camera, the light temporarily takes the place of the camera's shutter. Used in a dark room or outdoors at night, strobe lights can illuminate a moving object for as little as 1/1,000,000th of a second. By capturing the moving object at the moment it

Opposite
Harold Edgerton was able to capture the briefest moments, such as the instant when a droplet of milk creates a splash like a tiny fountain.

is lit, a photograph can reveal the smallest details of the fastest movements.

Another specialized use of cameras that helps us see the world in new ways is photomacrography, which enlarges small objects. Using special lenses and camera adaptations, an amateur photographer can photograph tiny insects, seedpods, or the rainbow-colored scales on a butterfly's wing, in all their detail. Scientists, however, go a step farther, using specially equipped cameras attached to microscopes. These cameras can capture images of minuscule crystals, animals, and plants, and even the cells that make up the human body. The scanning electron microscope — an even more refined microscope/camera combination — produces crystal-clear images that magnify the original as much as one million times. Even DNA, hidden within the living cell, can be seen and photographed with a scanning electron microscope.

From the earliest days of the camera, people tried to photograph the night sky and celestial objects visible there. The first well-documented daguerreotype of the moon was taken at the Harvard Observatory in 1851, the year that is generally considered the beginning of astronomical photography. Telescopes in modern observatories may be thought of as very special large cameras since they can only be used with a sensitized plate. For years, astronomers have been using electronically sensitized plates. By using long exposures, it is possible to record clear images of objects too faint for the human eye to see even with the most powerful telescopes available for direct viewing. The Hubble Space Telescope, which is fitted with numerous digital cameras, is a giant orbiting camera that has produced spectacular pictures of stars, planets, and nebulae. Similar and even more effective orbiting telescopes will certainly appear in the years to come.

In recent years special cameras fitted in steel housings have been lowered to the deepest depths in the world's oceans. Television cameras mounted in robot submarines helped discover the wreck of the *Titanic*. In the next century, we can expect underwater robot cameras to locate ships lost hundreds of years ago and to solve more mysteries about our oceans.

Opposite top
Specially equipped cameras can make the tiniest objects seem huge. When they are enlarged to this degree, red and white blood cells reveal their very different forms.

Opposite bottom
The most unimaginably enormous objects, such as the Spiral Nebula, which is about 100,000 light years across, can fit into a single photographic image.

Most cameras made for amateur photographers these days are "point-and-shoot" models, which contain a computer chip that automatically judges focus, exposure time, whether a flash is needed, and other necessary tasks.

Just over a decade ago, the first modern single-use, or disposable, camera made its appearance. These inexpensive cameras have been a huge success. It is estimated that nearly one-half of the snapshots taken annually are made with disposable cameras. Single-use cameras are constructed entirely with automatic machinery, using modern injection-molded plastics, high-quality plastic lenses, and improved color-negative films. They will continue to be improved, with more models available well into the next century.

Even more important is the arrival of digital cameras, which are operated by a chip that automatically and constantly monitors everything from whether the batteries have enough power to whether the chip itself is functioning properly. They also enable digital models to be the first cameras that operate without either film or photographic plates.

The heart of a digital camera is called a charge-coupled device (CCD). It is the CCD that takes the place of regular film – it records an image that it stores on a computer chip, a memory card, or in some models a regular disk of the type used with computers. Most models use a memory card, which can be erased and used repeatedly. The smallest card, a four-megabyte model, can store between sixty and one hundred images.

The image is stored as pixels, which are bits of red, green, or blue information lined up in rows on the CCD. When organized this way, the pixels are a form of code, much as written data is stored in binary code on a computer. The process of turning the pixels into a photograph starts with the pixels moving off the CCD, row by row. The image's colors are checked and corrected,

Disposable cameras, such as this Kodak Max, are inexpensive and easy to use. Instead of removing a roll of completed film, the photographer sends the entire camera to the developer, who removes and processes the film and recycles the rest of the camera.

and the pixels are rearranged to form a digital image, which is then added to either the camera's built-in storage or to the memory card.

In many digital models, you can view the pictures you've taken on a small screen. If you don't like the way an image looks, you can delete it immediately and try again. With this technology, you will never have to wait for an important roll of film to come back from the photo lab to see if your shots came out. It is now also possible to "date stamp" images (record when the picture was taken),

and at least one digital camera comes with a small microphone that allows you to record a six-second message to accompany every picture.

Having taken a series of photographs and returned home, you attach the camera to your computer and download the photographs you've taken. (One new invention makes the job even easier: A manufacturer has devised a small card, roughly the size and shape of a stick of chewing gum, that can store digital photographs, video, and audio. You simply pop it out of your digital camera and into your laptop computer.) Just a few minutes after you've snapped the shot, you can be viewing the image on your screen or transferring it to a CD, a kind of digital photo album, for long-term storage. Since the images are stored on the computer, they can easily be printed in homemade greeting cards, newsletters, E-mails, or other documents. The digital camera makes home publishing with photographs possible.

With a related innovation, you don't even have to transfer the image from a camera to a computer, because the two devices go everywhere together:

Just one of the new innovations transforming the camera: Photographers can jot down captions directly onto an image with an electronic pen that comes with this model.

There is now a one-and-a-half-inch-thick notebook computer on the market that comes equipped with a Pentium processor, a 4.3-gigabyte hard drive, and a digital camera, all in a package that weighs just two and a half pounds. You can snap a photograph and then sit right down and check out your shot on the computer screen.

Digital cameras put you in control of every step of the photographic process. You can even edit your photographs, transforming them with just a few clicks of the mouse. Using any one of several software packages, you can change someone's eyes from blue to green; remove unsightly buildings from an otherwise beautiful landscape; or even repair the crack in the Liberty Bell or give the Sphinx a nose. Where photographs once recorded the world with greater realism than any painting could match, now they can take on whatever reality you choose.

Predicting future trends is always difficult. Compared to traditional cameras, consumer digital cameras are still very expensive and the quality of the output is still below that of even inexpensive film cameras. But this is changing. At some point in the new century, it is reasonable to expect the price of digital cameras to drop to a point where more customers will find them an attractive alternative to traditional cameras.

The arrival of digital cameras has brought photography full circle. A gorgeous color image displayed on a computer screen may be a far cry from the first crude images produced by Niepce, Daguerre, or Talbot, but now, as then, the photographer is in complete control of the process. From the moment you snap a picture, through the moment that picture appears in its final form on your computer screen or printed out on paper, you are responsible for every step. Like the brilliant inventors who made today's cameras possible, you too can be a pioneer of photography.

Above
Today's cameras are remarkably versatile. This compact digital model, for example, can take both still photographs and video.

Opposite
With digital images and the right computer software, you can manipulate a photograph to suit your wildest imagination.

FURTHER READING

Auer, Michel. *The Illustrated History of the Camera*. Boston: New York Graphic Society, 1975.

Brayer, Elizabeth. *George Eastman*. Baltimore: Johns Hopkins University Press, 1996.

Coe, Brian. *The Birth of Photography*. New York: Taplinger, 1976.

Collins, Douglas. *The Story of Kodak*. New York: Harry N. Abrams, 1990.

Frizot, Michel, ed. *A New History of Photography*. Koln: Konemann Verlagsgesellschaft mbH, 1998.

Henisch, Heinz K. and Bridget A. Henisch. *The Photographic Experience 1839-1914: Images and Attitudes*. University Park, Pennsylvania: Pennsylvania University Press, 1994.

Goldberg, Vicki, ed. *Photography in Print*. New York: Touchstone, 1981.

Goldsmith, Arthur. *The Camera and Its Images*. New York: Ridge Press/ Newsweek Books, 1979.

Lucie-Smith, Edward. *The Invented Eye*. New York: Paddington Press, 1975.

Macdonald, Gus. *Camera: Victorian Eyewitness*. New York: Viking, 1980.

Newhall, Nancy. *From Adams to Stieglitz: Pioneers of Modern Photography*. New York: Aperture, 1999.

Ritchin, Fred. *In Our Own Image*. New York: Aperture, 1990.

Sandler, Martin W. *The Story of American Photography*. Boston: Little, Brown, 1979.

Swedlund, Charles. *Photography: A Handbook of History, Materials and Processes*. New York: Holt, Rinehart and Winston, 1974.

Time-Life (Editors of). *Color*. Alexandria, Virginia: Time-Life Books, 1981.

———. *Frontiers of Photography*. New York: Time-Life Books, 1972.

———. *Photography as a Tool*. Alexandria, Virginia: Time-Life Books, 1982.

INDEX

c

Produced by
CommonPlace Publishing
2 Morse Court
New Canaan, Connecticut 06840

The text and display for this book have been typeset in various weights and sizes of Futura. A sans serif face designed in Germany in 1928 by Paul Renner, Futura has been widely copied and adapted for digital type systems. Based upon geometric shapes, the Futura letter is characterized by lines of uniform width. Previous typefaces reflected the irregularities of hand lettering.

We wish to express our sincere gratitude to Morgan Wesson and especially to camera historian Philip L. Condax, whose expertise greatly enriched this book. The index was prepared by Elizabeth A. McCarthy.